Late Nite Comic

Book by
Allan Knee

Music and Lyrics by
Brian Gari

SAMUEL FRENCH

FOUNDED 1830

NEW YORK HOLLYWOOD LONDON TORONTO

SAMUELFRENCH.COM

Cover art by Roberto Gari

978-0-573-66242-3   Printed   in   U.S.A.   #13859

IMPORTANT BILLING AND CREDIT REQUIREMENTS

All producers of *LATE NITE COMIC must* give credit to the Author of the Play in all programs distributed in connection with performances of the Play, and in all instances in which the title of the Play appears for the purposes of advertising, publicizing or otherwise exploiting the Play and/or a production. The name of the Author *must* appear on a separate line on which no other name appears, immediately following the title and *must* appear in size of type not less than fifty percent of the size of the title type.

LATE NITE COMIC premiered at the Ritz Theatre on October 15, 1987. The Musical Director was Gregory J. Dlugos with the music Orchestrated by Larry Hochman, Vocal arrangements by James Raitt and Dance arrangements by James Raitt. The production was Directed by Philip Rose; Choreographed by Dennis Dennehy, with Scenic Design by Clarke Dunham, Lighting Design by Ken Billington, Costume Design by Gail Cooper-Hecht, Sound Design by Abe Jacob, the Projection Coordinator was Barbara Tumarkin Dunham, with Hair Design by Howard Leonard and Associate Lighting Design by John McKernon.

The Production Stage Manager was Mortimer Halpern, the Stage Manager was Brian A. Kaufman and Assistant Stage Manager Lorna Littleway, with the following cast:

DAVID ACKERMAN . . . . Robert LuPone
GABRIELLE . . . . Teresa Tracy
ENSEMBLE, SUSAN, HOOKER . . . . Pamela Blasetti
ENSEMBLE, CLUB OWNER, HOOKER . . . . Kim Freshwater
ENSEMBLE, JENNY, HOOKER . . . . Lauren Goler
ENSEMBLE, CECIL, CLUB OWNER,
VOICE OF GOD, KRAZY KORN EMCEE . . . . Patrick Hamilton
ENSEMBLE, HOOKER . . . . Judine Hawkins
ENSEMBLE, TANYA, DELILAH . . . . Aja Major
ENSEMBLE, CLUB OWNER, MIKE, LAS VEGAS EMCEE . . Michael McAssey
ENSEMBLE, HOOKER, METROPOLITAN BALLERINA . . . Sharon Moore
ENSEMBLE, NAT, BARTENDER, DAVID'S ALTER EGO . . . . Mason Roberts
ENSEMBLE, CLARA, HOOKER . . . . Susan Santoro
ENSEMBLE, CLUB OWNER, BARTENDER, BUSBOY . . . . Don Stitt
Swings: Danielle P. Connell, Barry Finkel.
Understudies: Patrick Hamilton (David Ackerman), Susan Santoro (Gabrielle).

CHARACTERS

DAVID ACKERMAN, a stand-up comic
GABRIELLE, a dancer
An **ENSEMBLE OF MEN AND WOMEN** in various roles

(In the Broadway production, the Ensemble was comprised of 7 Men and 4 Women, although the Ensemble can be effectively cast with as few as 3 Men and 3 Women, or expanded as desired.)

MUSICAL SYNOPSIS

The story is set in the present in various locations in New York City and, later, in Las Vegas. The conventions of time and place do not interrupt the flow of one scene into another.

ACT I

ACT II

Music 1: OVERTURE

Music la: CURTAIN

ACT I

Scene 1: A Piano Bar

(DAVID ACKERMAN, a young man, sits at a piano, playing, telling us his story. He is a seeker – direct, open, with no artifice about him. Much of his humor comes from his innocence.)

DAVID. Do you ever feel sometimes like you hadn't done anything right since puberty? Remember puberty? Remember studying your naked body and asking, "What the hell do I do with this?"

(He continues playing piano.)

But life goes on. Puberty came and went. You survived. But you didn't marry the sweetheart of your dreams. You didn't make a killing on the stock market. And you finally landed in a hellish little piano bar over in the West 40s.

(Lights up on a midtown piano lounge.)

Music 2: STAND UP

Of course you still have your dreams. And sometimes late at night, when the crowd settles into a drunken stupor, you quietly take hold of the mike. You let a little boldness into your heart. And you tell the joint what you really want to do.

I AM NOT YOUR PIANO MAN OR BILLY JOEL
I JUST WANNA BE A STAND UP

I FORGOT "UNFORGETTABLE" BY NAT KING COLE
I JUST WANNA BE A STAND UP
I AM NOT SINGING "MY WAY" FOR THE HUNDREDTH
TIME
I DON'T CARE IF YOU'VE GOT YOUR HAND UP
YOU CAN PUT IT DOWN 'CAUSE I'M GETTING UP
AND I'M GONNA BE A STAND UP!

(He comes forward.)

I AM NOT GONNA WAIT AROUND FOR DOLLAR TIPS
I AM GONNA BE A STAND UP
I'LL HIT THE "RISING STARS" AND THE "COMIC
STRIPS"
'CAUSE I'M GONNA BE A STAND UP
GET ANOTHER GUY – HIRE BASS AND DRUMS
IF YOU WANT YOU CAN BRING A BAND UP
BUT I'M COMING OUT FROM THE 88'S
AND I'M GONNA BE A STAND UP!
I'M THROUGH PLAYING HAROLD ARLEN
I'LL BE THE NEXT GEORGE CARLIN –

(The music continues under as he speaks.)

I'll tell you my dream of life. To be bi-coastal. To call
my folks on the phone and say, "Ma! Pa! I'm bi-coastal!"
That they'd understand. That they'd be proud of.
"Our son – our boy – is bi coastal." They'd march in
bi-coastal parades. They'd wear bi-coastal tee-shirts.
You don't have to tell them it's Tijuana and the South
Bronx. Folks don't want particulars. They want good
news. "You're happy – good. You're bi-coastal – terrific.
Just don't tell your grandparents."
I'LL BE AS HOT AS FIRE
IN FACT, LIKE RICHARD PRYOR.

AND I'M THROWIN' OUT ALL MY SONGBOOKS NOW
'CAUSE I'M GONNA BE A STAND UP
I DON'T NEED THAT STUFF 'CAUSE I MADE A VOW
THAT I'M GONNA BE A STAND UP
AND I'LL GET THAT SPOT ON A FRIDAY NIGHT
IF I CAN KEEP BUILDING THAT DEMAND UP

AND YOU'LL NEVER CATCH ME WHEN I'M SITTING
DOWN
'CAUSE I'LL ALWAYS BE A STAND UP
STAND UP!
STAND UP!

(He returns to the piano.)

You gotta be realistic, of course. You gotta earn a living.
So tonight you sit back and entertain the crowd with
some choice piano selections –

AM I BLUE?

Later you'll collect your tips – smile at everybody – and
go home. Maybe alone – maybe not. I've never had
much luck with women. It's not that I haven't tried.
You work these late-night clubs, you get a few golden
opportunities.

(He continues playing.)

Like one night I'm playing this bar – my mind is off in
a thousand different directions – when this crazy girl
starts talking to me.

*(A young, off-beat-looking woman – **GABRIELLE** – has
turned to him at the piano bar. She is very lively and
engaging.)*

GABRIELLE. I read lips...You were talking to yourself.

DAVID. Was I?

GABRIELLE. You were saying some pretty wild things. Am I
intruding?

DAVID. No –

GABRIELLE. You Armenian? You don't have to answer. It's
just that my astrologer said I'd meet an Armenian
who'd bring me good luck.

DAVID. I'm not Armenian. But I'm lucky.

GABRIELLE. God, it's a hot night.

DAVID. *(Front)* She does have a pretty face.

GABRIELLE. I'm a dancer.

DAVID. A dancer?

GABRIELLE. You couldn't tell? I know I don't have a dancer's look.

DAVID. Well, you do.

GABRIELLE. Well, I don't. Most dancers you look at them and know immediately – dancer. You look at Nureyev and you know immediately – dancer. You see that guy over there?

DAVID. Dancer?

GABRIELLE. *(Laughing)* No – no.

DAVID. No?

GABRIELLE. No, he's my date. I told him, "Cecil, no food – no drugs – no late nights – and no sex." You'd think I was talking to myself. He's pawing me. He's popping pills. He's getting me crazy. I keep telling myself, "Never again." And then, "never again" happens again. My name's Gabrielle.

DAVID. David.

GABRIELLE. Hi. I was born Janet. You don't see me as a Janet?

DAVID. Well, I –

GABRIELLE. No. No, I'm not a Janet. No. God, no. I saw this movie and there was this girl in it called Gabrielle. And everything she wanted, she got. I mean, she got everything. So I thought, "What's in a name?" He's looking over here. I find the strangest men. You could blindfold me – put me in a crowded room with just one maniac and I'd find him. You know Rodney Dangerfield?

DAVID. Rodney Dangerfield – sure.

GABRIELLE. He saw me dance. He was so nice. He said whenever I'm in town I should give him a call.

DAVID. Rodney Dangerfield wants you to call him?

GABRIELLE. The thing is this – I'm in town all the time. I live here. So I'm asking myself – what town is he talking about? Newark?

DAVID. Listen ... I'm a comic.

GABRIELLE. You?

DAVID. You couldn't tell?

GABRIELLE. I thought there was something funny about you.

DAVID. I've appeared in a few small clubs. Actually, I've done two street fairs and a Turkish bath. I'd give anything to meet Dangerfield.

GABRIELLE. Maybe I could arrange it.

(She looks at him; smiles.)

David.

DAVID. David, yes.

GABRIELLE. Like the king.

DAVID. Gabrielle. Like the dancer.

GABRIELLE. I better go. Cecil's about to go berserk. Thanks for the chat.

DAVID. Don't go. I enjoyed talking to you.

(He plays and sings as if he is spontaneously creating a song for her)

Music 3: GABRIELLE.

GABRIELLE, I DON'T KNOW WHERE YOU CAME FROM
GABRIELLE, WHERE DID YOU GET THAT NAME
FROM?
GABRIELLE, I DO AGREE THAT JANET
ISN'T RIGHT FOR YOU BUT CAN IT

CHANGE YOUR LIFE AND BRING YOU LUCK FOREVER
GABRIELLE, I'M TRYING TO BE CLEVER
GABRIELLE, I'M HAPPY THAT YOU BURST IN
MAYBE I COULD BE THE FIRST IN LINE
TO SEE YOUR SHOWS
I'LL BRING A ROSE
GABRIELLE, YOU'RE REALLY OFF THE WALL BUT
GABRIELLE, IT'S CRAZY IF I FALL BUT
GABRIELLE, YOU'RE THE PRETTIEST OF DANCERS
I CAN HELP YOU FIND YOUR ANSWERS
MAD'MOISELLE
MY GABRIELLE.

GABRIELLE. Thanks. That's nice.

(She sticks a bill in the glass on the piano.)

DAVID. Hey!

GABRIELLE. What?

DAVID. Don't.

GABRIELLE. You kidding? You practically saved my life tonight ... You got great eyes.

DAVID. Really? I never noticed.

(Front)

That's a lie. I have noticed.

GABRIELLE. See you.

DAVID. See you.

(She starts to go, then turns back.)

GABRIELLE. Bye.

DAVID. Bye.

(The club manager, **NAT,** *comes on.)*

NAT. Pack it in, Ackerman.

DAVID. Hey, Nat.

NAT. Yeah?

DAVID. You see that girl?

NAT. What girl?

DAVID. The one I was talking to.

NAT. Look, Ackerman, it's late. My feet are killing me. I'm so tired, I'm not even sure I'm awake.

(He goes. **DAVID** *continues front.)*

DAVID. So you meet this banana girl one night. You feel different. More alive. You leave the Piano Bar with all this energy. Every night after work I make a round of the Comedy Clubs – auditioning any act – hoping to hear somebody say those three magic words, "I like you."

Music 3a: *SCENE CHANGE*

Scene 2: Various Comedy Clubs

FIRST CLUB OWNER. O.K., babe. You got about five minutes.

DAVID. *(Performing)* How do you find a foreigner in N.Y.? ... Taxi.

How do you find an actor in N.Y.? ... Waiter!

How do you find a politician in N.Y.? ... Sing Sing.

Music 4: THE BEST IN THE BUSINESS

FIRST CLUB OWNER.

NO I'M SORRY WE DON'T NEED ANOTHER COMIC
HERE
WE DON T HAVE ROOM TO TAKE ANOTHER CHANCE
AND EVEN THOUGH I'VE NEVER HEARD YOUR ACT
BEFORE
I'LL GIVE YOU EV'RY PUNCH LINE IN ADVANCE.

'CAUSE YOU SEE I'M THE BEST IN THE BUSINESS
I CAN PICK 'EM OUT BEFORE THEY EVEN SPEAK!
YES YOU KNOW I'M THE BEST IN THE BUSINESS
....AND I'VE ONLY BEEN IN BUSINESS FOR A WEEK!

SECOND CLUB OWNER. *(Tough and cynical)* O.K., pal, make me laugh.

DAVID. *(Front)* If this guy laughed, his face would fall off.

SECOND CLUB OWNER. So what do you do?

DAVID. I do impressions. Wanna hear my impression of Michael Jackson? He's a good singer. Nice guy. Face keeps changing. That's just my impression.

SECOND CLUB OWNER.

NO, I'M SORRY WE DON'T NEED ANOTHER COMIC
HERE
UNLESS YOU WANNA WAIT ON LINE
THERE AREN'T VERY MANY GUYS AHEAD OF YOU
YOU'RE NUMBER'S PROB'LY NINETY-NINE.

FIRST & SECOND CLUB OWNERS.

'CAUSE YOU SEE WE'RE THE BEST IN THE BUSINESS
WE GOT ALL THE FUNNY GUYS IN TOWN YOU LIKE

YES, YOU KNOW WE'RE THE BEST IN THE BUSINESS –

SECOND CLUB OWNER.

COULD YOU SPEAK UP LOUD, I HAVEN'T BOUGHT A
MIKE!

THIRD CLUB OWNER. *(Ethnic street-type.)* You got anything a
little more traditional, kid?

DAVID. Traditional? Yeah, I think I do.

(Performing)

I grew up in a big Italian family. Eighteen kids. We put
my mom up on a pedestal – to keep her away from my
dad.

THIRD CLUB OWNER. No, ethnic jokes, huh!

DAVID. I got one you'll like –

THIRD CLUB OWNER.

NO, I'M SORRY WE DON'T NEED ANOTHER COMIC
HERE
I GOTTA RUN, I DON'T GOT TIME TO GAB
BUT YOU CAN ALWAYS ORDER FOOD AND HAVE A
DRINK
THE WAITRESSES WILL PUT IT ON YOUR TAB.

FIRST, SECOND & THIRD CLUB OWNERS.

'CAUSE YOU KNOW WE'RE THE BEST IN THE
BUSINESS
WE KNOW HOW TO MAKE A BUCK, YOU BET YOUR
LIFE
MAKING MONEY ISN'T FUNNY IT'S A BUSINESS –

THIRD CLUB OWNER.

JOHNNY CARSON COMES IN FREE, BUT NOT HIS
WIFE!

(The **FOURTH CLUB OWNER** *is a tall woman dressed
in hot leather pants and holding a whip. She is a sight
to behold.)*

FOURTH CLUB OWNER. C'mon, you got an act or you ain't
got an act?

DAVID. *(Performing)* The economy's so tight lately, even the
prostitutes are giving bargain rates. I saw this one lady

with a sign pinned to her breast. "Buy one, get the other free!"

FOURTH CLUB OWNER.

NO, I'M SORRY WE DON'T NEED ANOTHER COMIC HERE

WE'VE HAD OUR SHARE, WE DON'T NEED ANY MORE

BUT EVEN THOUGH WE'VE SEEN A MILLION GUYS LIKE YOU

OUR POLICY IS STILL AN OPEN DOOR.

ALL CLUB OWNERS.

'CAUSE YOU KNOW WE'RE THE BEST IN THE BUSINESS

WE CAN TELL A JOKE LIKE ONLY BERLE CAN DO

YES, YOU KNOW WE'RE THE BEST IN THE BUSINESS –

FOURTH CLUB OWNER.

WE'RE SO GOOD WE SHOULD BE UP THERE 'STEAD OF YOU!

(*The* **CLUB OWNERS** *dance.*)

ALL CLUB OWNERS.

'CAUSE YOU KNOW WE'RE THE BEST IN THE BUSINESS

WE CAN TELL A JOKE LIKE ONLY BERLE CAN DO

YES, YOU KNOW WE'RE THE BEST IN THE BUSINESS

WE'RE SO GOOD WE SHOULD BE UP THERE 'STEAD OF YOU!

WE'RE THE BEST, WE DON'T NEED YOU!

Scene 3: Alphabet City

(**DAVID** *is alone onstage.*)

DAVID. You leave your picture, say goodnight and go home. I live over on Avenue A. Not exactly the class part of town. But it's got character. A kind of open hostility. New York's the only place where it's perfectly natural to be angry.

(*He acts like a tough.*)

"Screw you, bud!"

(*Answering*)

"Anytime. Sure thing." But there's beauty here too. Like that girl. I mean where do you have encounters like that? And the birds. The birds are wild in this city.

(*To a bird.*)

"Hello, Lenny." My favorite – Lenny. We been going together – "How long's it been, Lenny? Two years? – that long?" By the time I reach home, I'm exhausted. I fall into bed and dream of me and Johnny Carson sitting side by side.

(*To Johnny.*)

"Well, John, I've got a two picture deal with Paramount. And there's talk of a series in the fall."

(*Front*)

It's one of those dreams you think to yourself, "Please, God, let me not wake from this one." And just as you're about to collect your award for Comic of the Year, someone bursts through the door and says –

Scene 4: David's Apartment

(It is dawn. GABRIELLE *has dropped in on him un-expectedly.)*

GABRIELLE. Hi. It's me. It's late, I know. Actually, it's almost morning.

(She sees he is half-asleep.)

I woke you up –

DAVID. No –

GABRIELLE. I did. I'm terribly sorry. I'll go –

(She turns to leave.)

DAVID. Come back!

(She turns back.)

GABRIELLE. Gabrielle.

DAVID. I know. Come in.

GABRIELLE. You sure?

DAVID. Come in.

(She comes in as he puts on his pants.)

GABRIELLE. Small world, isn't it?

DAVID. How'd you find me?

GABRIELLE. I went back to your club. I told what's his name — ?

DAVID. Nat.

GABRIELLE. I said I was carrying your child.

DAVID. You told him what?

GABRIELLE. He said it didn't surprise him. You live here?

DAVID. Yeah?

GABRIELLE. Alone? Look, you don't have to answer. But if you have someone, I'll go.

DAVID. I live alone.

GABRIELLE. Good. I mean, it's not that you shouldn't have someone. I just don't think – and it's a very quick observation – I don't think you're ready. I've insulted you –

DAVID. No –

GABRIELLE. I have. Look, I'll go –

DAVID. Calm down.

GABRIELLE. O.K.

DAVID. Have a seat.

GABRIELLE. I will.

> *(She sits.)*

Guess what.

DAVID. What?

GABRIELLE. I got a job dancing.

DAVID. Oh, yeah?

GABRIELLE. With Jerry Jerome. You know him?

DAVID. Jerry Jerome? – no.

GABRIELLE. He works the suburbs. He's very big in New Rochelle. Comes on like gang busters with the society ladies. They all wanna mother him or something. The last thing I'd wanna do is mother Jerry Jerome.

DAVID. What do you wanna do?

GABRIELLE. I wanna do something that'll knock people's heads off. I wanna be the most incredible ballerina that ever lived. Listen, what do you think of Romaine?

DAVID. Romaine?

GABRIELLE. Gabrielle Romaine. I'm trying it out. Pavlova. Fonteyn. And Gabrielle Romaine. It's catchy, huh?

DAVID. It sounds like a salad.

GABRIELLE. A salad?

DAVID. *(Calling)* "Hey, one Gabrielle Romaine and holda the dressing!"

GABRIELLE. Romaine is not the name I'm looking for.

> *(She gets up and moves about.)*

I was thinking to myself on the way over – what if he has a girl? Or what if he has a guy? I mean, you never know what you're gonna find. A sexy fellow like you.

DAVID. You think I'm sexy?

GABRIELLE. It's not obvious or anything. You're the type
   of guy someone could know for years and not even
   notice. And then one day you look up, and it's like a
   firecracker there.

DAVID. *(Front)* A part of me was thinking, "Get rid of this
   girl."

   (Turning to her.)

   So where you dancing?

GABRIELLE. Garden City.

DAVID. *(Front)* But another part was saying, "This is really
   very nice."

GABRIELLE. Then a matinee in Syosset. Two nights in
   Nyack. And a special benefit next Sunday in Paramus,
   New Jersey. You're welcome to come.

DAVID. Thanks.

GABRIELLE. I know it's not the Metropolitan Opera House.
   That's where I dream of dancing. With a full orchestra.
   A hundred violins. A follow-spot on me. And a line of
   men a mile long coming out afterwards with bouquets
   of roses. Sounds good.

DAVID. Sounds very good.

GABRIELLE. It was all Clara and I ever talked about.

DAVID. Who's Clara?

GABRIELLE. My first dance teacher. A sensational lady. If it
   wasn't for her, I'd never have become a dancer. She
   danced in Europe. For kings and queens. She knew
   Nijinsky. She knew everybody.

DAVID. Where'd you find her?

GABRIELLE. In the Yellow Pages. It's the only thing I've ever
   found in the Yellow Pages. "Dance like you've never
   known it." Immediately I knew it was for me.

Music 5: CLARA'S DANCING SCHOOL

UP ON THE CORNER OF A HUNDRED AND SIXTH
STREET
I WENT TO A DANCING SCHOOL

RUN BY A LADY, A LADY NAMED CLARA
AND SHE WASN'T ANYONE'S FOOL
'CAUSE SHE TAUGHT HER CLASSES
FOR LESS THAN A DOLLAR
AND SOMETIMES SHE TAUGHT FOR FREE
FOR SOME GIRLS THE CLASSES HAD SO LITTLE
MEANING
BUT THEY SURE MEANT THE WORLD TO ME.

'CAUSE I LEARNED ABOUT DANCING
AND I LEARNED ABOUT TOUR JETES
AND I KNOW THAT IT CHANGED MY LIFE
IN MANY WAYS, THOSE EARLY DAYS.

THE CLASS WASN'T BIG
AND CLARA WAS TINY
AND I WASN'T TALL MYSELF
AND I READ EVERY BOOK ALL ABOUT BALLERINAS
THAT CLARA HAD ON HER SHELF.
AND THEN THERE WERE TIMES
WHEN I JUST COULDN'T TAKE IT
AND EVERY PLIE TURNED OUT WRONG
BUT CLARA WOULD TAKE ME
TO SEE "SLEEPING BEAUTY"
AND I WANTED TO DANCE ALL NIGHT LONG.

'CAUSE I LEARNED ABOUT DANCING
AND I LEARNED ABOUT TOUR JETES
AND I KNOW THAT IT CHANGED MY LIFE
IN MANY WAYS, THOSE EARLY DAYS.

AND THEN CAME THE TIME
WHEN I SAID I WAS LEAVING
AND CLARA AND I WERE IN TEARS
AND SHE SPOKE ONCE AGAIN
OF THE ROSES AND ENCORES
AND ALL OF THE BEAUTIFUL YEARS.
AND NOW AS I GET TO A HUNDRED AND SIXTH
STREET
I NEVER FORGET TO STOP
AND PICTURE THE PLACE

WHERE I DID MY FIRST SOLO
THAT NOW IS A BARBERSHOP.

'CAUSE I LEARNED ABOUT DANCING
AND I LEARNED ABOUT TOUR JETES
AND I KNOW THAT IT CHANGED MY LIFE
IN MANY WAYS, THOSE EARLY DAYS
WITH CLARA.

GABRIELLE. Hey, I didn't tell you. I called Rodney Danger-field.

DAVID. You did?

GABRIELLE. His secretary said he'll get back to me. I won't hold my breath. Rodney Dangerfield – I mean, big deal.

DAVID. Of course it's a big deal. One gig at Dangerfield's and you practically got it made.

GABRIELLE. I'm 24 years old — a quarter of a century practi-cally – and I'm always looking elsewhere. I mean, how do I know right here, right now, life isn't going on?

DAVID. *(Front)* I felt like making love to her right then and there.

GABRIELLE. I bet you thought I was older than 24?

DAVID. You, I thought you were even younger.

GABRIELLE. I've got a youthful quality about me. Some say it's just immaturity. But I think some people live young. Oh, my God! Look at the time! I've got to get to rehearsal. Jerry Jerome goes bananas when I'm late.

(She collects her things hurriedly.)

DAVID. Will I see you again?

GABRIELLE. Yes, of course. I was hoping to spend a few nights here –

DAVID. Here?

GABRIELLE. Things got a little hairy where I was staying. Look if you'd rather I didn't

DAVID. No, I –

GABRIELLE. I can see you're put out. I can go to a hotel –

DAVID. A hotel?

GABRIELLE. There's one down the street –

DAVID. I wouldn't hear of it –

GABRIELLE. No?

DAVID. No! You'll stay here.

GABRIELLE. I'm not looking for anything meaningful or lasting, you understand.

DAVID. You don't have to explain. Cheap and insignificant is really fine for me.

(Front)

I can't believe I said that.

GABRIELLE. You're really a very appealing person.

DAVID. I work at it.

GABRIELLE. You're obviously very successful in your work.

(She looks at him, smiles.)

Ciao.

(She goes.)

DAVID. Ciao.

(Front)

I know. Insanity. You don't open your doors and invite strangers to live with you. These decisions in life you gotta give thought to. You go out on a date. You got out on several dates. You go bowling. You let her beat you bowling. You take a bike ride. You push her off the bike 'cause she beat you bowling. You read your astrological chart. You consult your shrink. Then you have your disaster ... She said I was sexy. I mean, big deal. I'm a grown man. Do compliments affect me? Yes. Yes, they do. It's madness. It'll be like all the others. Melody. And Maria. And Pam. And Carrie –

Scene 5: David's Apartment

(**GABRIELLE** *enters with all her belongings. She and* **DAVID** *are very awkward with each other, wondering if they made the right decision.*)

GABRIELLE. I'm here.

DAVID. Hi.

GABRIELLE. Am I late?

DAVID. No.

GABRIELLE. Moving's such a pain.

DAVID. Yeah, I know.

GABRIELLE. Where should I put my things?

DAVID. Anywhere.

(*Front*)

What am I doing?

Music 6: THIS LADY ISN'T RIGHT FOR ME

DAVID. (*With gusto.*)
REMEMBER TANYA
SHE'D LAY IT ON YA
SHE REALLY GAVE ME QUITE A WHIRL
IN BED SHE THRILLED ME
BUT THEN WHAT KILLED ME
SHE LEFT ME FOR ANOTHER GIRL.
AND I SWORE UP AND DOWN
THERE WAS NO WAY SHE COULD EVER BE
BUT HERE I AM AGAIN
THIS LADY ISN'T RIGHT FOR ME!

REMEMBER JENNY
IN LOVE WITH LENNY
SHE TOLD ME THINGS WERE GOING BAD
I TRIED TO HOLD HER
SHE LIKES 'EM OLDER
SO NOW SHE'S DATING LENNY'S DAD
AND I SWORE UP AND DOWN
THAT SHE WAS GONNA CHANGE HER MIND

BUT HERE I AM AGAIN
AND I KNOW WHAT I'M GONNA –

FINDING SOMEONE LIKE GABBY
WAS SUCH A WONDROUS THING
WINDING UP WITH A GIRL LIKE GABBY –

(Music stops abruptly.)

GABRIELLE. It's real nice of you to let me stay here.

DAVID. How long you planning to stay?

GABRIELLE. Why you have someone else coming in?

DAVID. *(Laughing)* No – no. Everybody's on a month-to-month lease.

GABRIELLE. I only meant – like a relative. Like a mother.

DAVID. She got married and got her own place. That was thirty years ago.

GABRIELLE. Oh.

*(She smiles as **DAVID** continues singing.)*

DAVID.
NO, IT'S JUST A FLING.

REMEMBER SUSAN
ALWAYS BOOZIN'
AND I'D BE PICKIN' UP THE TAB
IT GOT HER LOOSER
THOUGHT I'D SEDUCE HER
INSTEAD SHE THREW UP IN THE CAB
AND I SWORE UP AND DOWN
IT WAS REALLY ALMOST GUARANTEED
BUT HERE I AM AGAIN
THIS LADY ISN'T WHAT I –
NEEDING SOMEONE LIKE GABBY ISN'T SO BAD AT
ALL
NEEDING SOMEONE WHO'S SO APPEALING ...
THIS TIME I WON'T FALL

HERE I AM AGAIN
HERE I AM AGAIN
HERE I AM AGAIN
THIS LADY ISN'T RIGHT FOR ...

Gabrielle moved in the next day!

Scene 6: David's Apartment

(**DAVID** *comes down front and speaks to the audience.*)

DAVID. She wasn't like anyone I ever knew. Whatever the past was, this was different. We took walks. We took long walks. We took short walks. We walked to Battery Park. We walked across Central Park at night. Well, actually, that was more of a run. We'd walk to see who was playing at the comedy clubs. We'd go by Lincoln Center and she'd stare at the Met. On a street corner she'd suddenly start dancing. And in no time she'd have a crowd around her – everyone clapping. And she gave me the hat to hold to collect the money. The pay wasn't bad. And she had a thing about churches. She loved churches.

(*The lights come up to reveal David's apartment.* **GABRIELLE** *has entered in a wild mood. She starts taking off her things, throwing them around.*)

GABRIELLE. It's closed. Churches should never be closed. It's sacrilegious to close a church. You need a spiritual uplift. You see a church. You think, "Thank God, a church." You run up the steps – happy – hope pouring into your heart. And then you see a sign. "Church closed." You know what that means – "church closed?"

DAVID. No.

GABRIELLE. It means God is out to lunch.

(*She collapses on the bed or floor.*)

I'd give anything to dance in a place with a real dance floor – and a dressing room I can actually dress in. And a mirror where I can actually see myself. And a partner who doesn't get my body all bent out of shape. Squeeze my muscles 'til they're sore –

(*He starts to massage her.*)

DAVID. (*Front*) I loved massaging her.

GABRIELLE. Oh, yes, yes. That's nice. God, you got great fingers. It feels terrific having a real place to live in.

DAVID. Where are you from?

GABRIELLE. I was born in Cincinnati. The all-American family. Hard to believe, huh? My mom collects dishes and things like that. My dad's always had this thing about me being Miss America. When I was little, I'd walk around the house in this long gown with a crown on my head, carrying flowers and waving to everybody, while he sang, "There she is, Miss America – " I still choke up every time I see the Miss America contest. I half expect they're gonna call out my name.

(She turns to him.)

So how come?

DAVID. How come what?

GABRIELLE. How come you don't put the make on me?

DAVID. *(Front)* I knew I was forgetting something.

GABRIELLE. Most guys –

DAVID. I'm not most guys.

GABRIELLE. Maybe you don't like me.

DAVID. What are you talking about?

GABRIELLE. I'd understand if you didn't. Not everybody takes to me –

DAVID. You want me to make love to you?

GABRIELLE. No – no! God, no!

DAVID. *(Front)* Well, we settled that.

GABRIELLE. I was just curious. Sex just spoils things anyway. Gets everybody crazy. Believe me, I know, I've had experiences.

DAVID. You have?

GABRIELLE. Oh, yes.

DAVID. How many?

GABRIELLE. Well, a few. Most of them were terrible. Still I've had them. How about you?

DAVID. Me? Once.

GABRIELLE. Once? Just once?

DAVID. Maybe twice. I wasn't sure. It was dark.

GABRIELLE. You're lying.

DAVID. *(Smiling)* I like touching.

GABRIELLE. Touching's nice. Drives me crazy sometimes.

DAVID. I like people's bodies.

GABRIELLE. Bodies are incredible. You know there are no two bodies alike – isn't that something? Everybody's got a unique body.

DAVID. What's your ideal body?

GABRIELLE. I don't know if I have an ideal.

DAVID. Sure you do. Everybody does.

GABRIELLE. You got a nice body.

DAVID. *(Laughing)* Me?

GABRIELLE. You're very sensual. David, I don't wanna fall for you.

DAVID. I don't blame you.

GABRIELLE. You're not my type.

DAVID. I understand. I'm not my type.

GABRIELLE. I'm serious. I want things to stay just as they are.

(She lies back, happily.)

DAVID. *(Front)* Sometimes I just loved to look at her.

GABRIELLE. I really like it here.

DAVID. You're very beautiful.

GABRIELLE. No –

DAVID. You are.

GABRIELLE. You really think I'm beautiful?

DAVID. Yes, I do.

GABRIELLE. I don't like my face.

DAVID. Of course, it's not a Miss America face. Your eyes are too small – and your nose is too big – and you've got spaces between your teeth –

GABRIELLE. *(Covering her face.)* God, I'm a mess.

DAVID. *(With care.)* I crown you Miss America.

(He puts an imaginary crown on her head. She looks

up; he kisses her.)

GABRIELLE. You got nice lips.

(They kiss again.)

GABRIELLE. You can tell a lot about a person by the way he kisses.

DAVID. What can you tell about me?

GABRIELLE. I think your life's going to go through a monumental change.

DAVID. *(Front)* It was the best news I had in years.

(They kiss again.)

GABRIELLE. Look, I got a confession. I suffer from post-coital depression.

DAVID. That's O.K. I suffer from pre-coital anxiety.

GABRIELLE. Oh, good.

(They kiss again, passionately.)

Scene 7: The Piano Bar and the Street

(**DAVID** *is alone onstage. He comes down front, a smile of satisfaction on his face.*)

DAVID. It was a night to remember. And it only got better. She was right about my life. It was changing. I was taller. Tougher. I had a new attitude. In fact, I no longer had an attitude.

(*He goes and sits at his piano.*)

Things that used to irritate me – nothing. People that used to intimidate me – friendly and sweet.

(*He waves at an angry-looking face.*)

Hi.

(*The* **MAN** *spits.*)

Guy's got a little congestion problem.

(*A* **WOMAN** *brushes past him. She spills her drink on him.*)

WOMAN. You stupid jerk, you think you own the place!

DAVID. It's yours. I give it to you.

(*Front*)

I'll tell you, when you're feeling good – it's amazing how little things don't mean a lot.

(**ANOTHER WOMAN** *and a* **MAN** *are in the midst of a fight.*)

MAN. I'll see you in hell.

ANOTHER WOMAN. It's the only place you will see me.

(*She slugs him.* **DAVID** *sings, simply, lovingly, while all around him frenetic activity goes on.*)

Music 7: *NOTHING'S CHANGING THIS LOVE*

DAVID.

THE CITY LOOKS GREAT TO ME –

(*A* **WOMAN** *blows smoke in his face.*)

POLLUTION I JUST CAN"T SEE
THE GARBAGE TRUCK'S MAKIN' NOISE
IT'S NOW JUST ONE OF MY JOYS
I'D SAY IT'S MUSIC TO MY EARS

SANITATION MAN. *(Shouting)* Hey, Jack, over here!

*(Garbage is thrown right past **DAVID**'s face.)*

DAVID.

'CAUSE NOTHING'S CHANGIN' MY MOOD
NOTHING'S CHANGIN' MY MIND
NOTHING'S CHANGIN' THIS LOVE I FIND.

(The sound of a screeching subway car.)

THE SUBWAY — IT'S RUNNING LATE
DON'T MIND IT — I LIKE THE WAIT
THE PLACE IS HOTTER THAN HELL
I'M SURE ENJOYING THE SMELL
I THINK I'LL HAVE MY LUNCH DOWN HERE –

AND NOTHING'S CHANGIN' MY MOOD
NOTHING'S CHANGIN' MY MIND
NOTHING'S CHANGIN' THIS LOVE I FIND.

(The sound of car horns.)

THE CARS OUTSIDE ARE HONKING CONSTANTLY
TO ME IT SOUNDS LIKE FOUR-PART HARMONY-

*(A **MUGGER** frisks him.)*

THE CITY IS FULL OF FEARS
THE MUGGERS – I BUY 'EM BEERS

(Calling)

On the house!

MY LANDLORD TURNED OFF THE HEAT
HE WANTS ME OUT ON THE STREET
I THINK I'LL KISS HIM ON THE LIPS.
'CAUSE NOTHING'S CHANGIN' MY MOOD
NOTHING'S CHANGIN' MY MIND
NOTHING'S CHANGIN' THIS LOVE I FIND!

Scene 8: The Piano Bar

(GABRIELLE enters and sits next to him on the piano bench.)

GABRIELLE. There were two hundred girls there. I think half the girls in the city are dancers. I figured I'd do O.K., though. I had this incredible energy. In my head, I'm doing all the routines. I'm leaping – Going up in the air – and stopping. Anyway, my turn finally comes. I step forward. I'm ready to knock their socks off — when this guy comes out and says, "That's it, girls. No more for today."

DAVID. You didn't get to dance?

GABRIELLE. Well, actually, I did. I told 'em, "Fellas, look, I've come to dance and I'm going to dance. I've been waiting over three hours." So – I just started dancing. You would have been proud of me, David. I was as light as a feather, leaping and spinning. I was terrific. That's what the security guards said.

DAVID. Security guards?

GABRIELLE. The two who ushered me out. Really sweet guys. They said without question, I was the best dancer that day. Anyway – it wasn't much of a company. I don't know what I was getting myself all excited about.

(She gets up.)

DAVID. Where you going?

GABRIELLE. I need a walk.

DAVID. Stick around, I get off soon.

GABRIELLE. No – I need to be alone, David. I need to do some thinking.

DAVID. Hey, we always walk together.

GABRIELLE. We don't always walk together. Sometimes we walk apart.

DAVID. You meeting someone?

GABRIELLE. No – I'm just going for a walk.

DAVID. What about dinner?

GABRIELLE. Why all these questions?

DAVID. I just wanna know where you're going.

GABRIELLE. I told you – for a walk.

DAVID. *(Front)*

(She crosses and puts her arms around him from behind.)

Yesterday I was coming down Lexington Avenue and I saw her. I almost didn't recognize her. She looked fantastic. Suddenly I got this crazy idea to follow her –

GABRIELLE. You followed me?

DAVID. Just a few blocks. It was just a game.

GABRIELLE. A game? David, that's not a game.

DAVID. Not really a game, I know. I had this idea of coming up behind you –

GABRIELLE. I'm going –

DAVID. *(Calling after her.)* Who was the guy?

GABRIELLE. What guy?

DAVID. You met a guy.

GABRIELLE. I didn't meet a guy.

DAVID. Yes, you did. You met a guy. I know a guy when I see a guy. Look, I'm not the jealous type

GABRIELLE. You are the jealous type.

DAVID. Well, O.K., I am the jealous type –

GABRIELLE. That was my daddy!

DAVID. *(Taken aback.)* Your daddy?

GABRIELLE. He wanted to see how his little Miss America was doing.

DAVID. Your daddy ... He's very attractive.

GABRIELLE. Yeah.

DAVID. What'd you do?

GABRIELLE. We had lunch. We talked. He's worried about me.

DAVID. Is he?

GABRIELLE. He's worried about me being in New York and getting nowhere. And living with a comic who should be getting his own act together instead of following after me ... I'll see you later. *(She goes.)*

Scene 9: A Comedy Club

(DAVID is alone onstage.)

DAVID. She was right. What was I doing – following people about? What was I becoming? Was I gonna stay a piano player all my life? That night I went to every comedy club on the circuit. I felt confident, ready for something. I was going to be direct, firm and hilarious. I wasn't gonna quit till they heard me. I kept at it till three in the morning. I was just about to join the Foreign Legion when I noticed I was standing in front of Krazy Korn, one of the hot new Comedy Clubs. So I decided – all right, last shot.

(A voice calls out.)

VOICE (OFFSTAGE). Who are you?

DAVID. *(Nervous)* I'm David Ackerman. I do stand-up. I know it's a little late. I don't know how I got here. The last thing I remember, I was looking for my cat and I fell down this hole –

(Brief pause.)

Hear about the philandering husband who comes home late one night? He undresses quietly to avoid waking his wife. But she's watching him through these half closed eyes. Suddenly she cries out, "Henry, where is your underwear?" He freezes, looks down, screams, "My God, I've been robbed!"

(Brief pause.)

I told my girl friend that. She thought it was hilarious. Couldn't stop laughing.

(He relaxes.)

I got a new girl friend. Real nice. Things are going great. Well, pretty good anyway. Trouble is I can't sleep at night. Albert Schweitzer only slept three hours and he did O.K. And they say Einstein didn't sleep at all. So who knows? ... But we got some interesting things going for us. Like lovemaking. It's not just making love. It's like a "happening." Even our kisses are an adventure. We got tongue positions that would surprise even Dr. Ruth. And we take risks. We make love in movie theaters – in taxis – once on top of the Empire State Building. Sure I was nervous. At that height? ... I keep hearing sex is overrated. If it is, can you imagine where everything else stands? ... But sex isn't the whole thing. Not by a long shot. It's like I'm becoming a new person. My teeth are getting sharper. And I've got hair on my fingertips. And when the moon is full, I turn purple ...

(*He smiles.*)

I think you get the picture. Sometimes I find myself talking non-stop – like I'm talking right now. I talk about anything. Stupid things. Like the fact there are millions of galaxies in the universe and only ours plays baseball –

VOICE (OFFSTAGE). I like you.

DAVID. You like me?

VOICE (OFFSTAGE). You're different.

DAVID. Well, thanks. It's a nice place here.

VOICE (OFFSTAGE). How's Monday?

DAVID. Monday?

VOICE (OFFSTAGE). Monday night.

DAVID. What about it?

VOICE (OFFSTAGE). You wanna work?

DAVID. Do I wanna work?

VOICE (OFFSTAGE). Do you?

DAVID. Do I?

VOICE (OFFSTAGE). I gotta spot for you.

DAVID. You gotta spot for me?

VOICE (OFFSTAGE). Stop repeating everything I way.

DAVID. O.K.

VOICE (OFFSTAGE). I'll see you Monday.

DAVID. I'll see you Monday – yeah.

(Front)

I couldn't believe it. You know what it's like when something happens you've been waiting for all your life? You become humble, submissive, contrite. You fall to your knees

(He falls to his knees.)

You thank God for all His little blessings. And you say simply

Music 8: *Reprise – BEST IN THE BUSINESS*

(Slowly rising.)

AND YOU KNOW I'M THE BEST IN THE BUSINESS
AND I'M STAYIN' IN THIS BUSINESS TILL I DROP
YES, YOU KNOW I'M THE BEST IN THE BUSINESS
AND I'M GOING TO MAKE IT TO THE VERY TOP!

Scene 10: David's Apartment

(**GABRIELLE** *moves about*. **DAVID** *is excited*.)

DAVID. I went to these four or five places – and nothing. And I mean nothing. You'd have thought I was giving a eulogy at a funeral.

(*Performing*)

But I wouldn't quit. I'd think of you. I'd get all excited and march into the next club –

(*Strong*)

"Ackerman here!" – And I was fine. Finally I saw this guy from Krazy Korn. I figured this would be my last stop of the day, I'd give it all I got. I don't know what inspired me, but I started talking about us.

GABRIELLE. About us?

DAVID. I told him about us. The crazy things we'd do. I don't know, maybe I was just worn out from trying so hard – but I relaxed and talked. It felt good. Guess what?

GABRIELLE. What?

DAVID. He liked me. I'm going to be appearing there – next Monday.

GABRIELLE. You're kidding?

DAVID. No. David Ackerman has a real job.

(*Performing as an M.C.*)

"Let's give a warm welcome to the kid from Avenue A!"

(*He cheers.*)

GABRIELLE. It's weird, but I had a feeling this was going to be a good day for you.

DAVID. I reserved a table for you.

GABRIELLE. For me?

DAVID. Ringside. And I'm having a limousine pick you up. I'm going to get you a gown. I saw this gold lame thing in the window over on East Fifth. A beauty –

GABRIELLE. David, don't count on me.

DAVID. What do you mean, don't count on you? I couldn't do this without you. Hey, this is what we've been talking about.

Music 9: IT HAD TO HAPPEN SOMETIME

> I JUST COULDN'T WAIT TO TELL YOU
> THIS IS LIKE A DREAM COME TRUE
> WHAT I'VE ALWAYS WANTED'S FIN'LLY COMING
> THROUGH.
>
> WELL, IT HAD TO HAPPEN SOMETIME
> MY FUTURE IS CLEAR
> YES, IT HAD TO HAPPEN SOMETIME
> AND IT'S FINALLY HERE
> 'CAUSE SOMETIMES YOU WAKE UP
> AND THINGS CHANGE SOMEHOW
> AND THAT SOMETIME JUST HAPPENS TO BE NOW.

GABRIELLE.

> THIS IS VERY HARD TO TELL YOU
> I AM NOT YOUR DREAM COME TRUE
> I COULD NEVER MAKE YOU HAPPY, THOUGHT YOU
> KNEW.
>
> WELL, IT HAD TO HAPPEN SOMETIME
> THERE'S NO TELLING WHEN
> IT HAD TO HAPPEN SOMETIME
> THAT TIME'S HERE AGAIN
> 'CAUSE SOMETIMES YOU WAKE UP
> AND THINGS CHANGE SOMEHOW
> AND THAT SOMETIME JUST HAPPENS TO BE NOW.

DAVID. The room isn't very big, but that's O.K. It's got a good ambience –

GABRIELLE.

> CAN'T YOU HEAR ONE WORD I'M SAYING?
> THERE'S JUST NO WAY I'LL BE STAYING

DAVID.

> WONDER WHAT THEY WILL BE PAYING.

DAVID. (CONT)

    I'LL WORK FOR NOTHING IF THEY WANT.

GABRIELLE.

    I AM SURE YOU'LL FIND ANOTHER.

DAVID.

    WONDER IF THEY'LL ASK FOR MORE.

GABRIELLE.

    DON'T YOU UNDERSTAND, I'M ALMOST OUT THE
    DOOR?

BOTH.

    WELL, IT HAD TO HAPPEN SOMETIME
    THERE'S NO TELLING WHEN
    IT HAD TO HAPPEN SOMETIME
    THAT TIME'S HERE AGAIN
    'CAUSE SOMETIMES YOU WAKE UP
    AND THINGS CHANGE SOMEHOW
    AND THAT SOMETIME JUST HAPPENS TO BE –

GABRIELLE.

    DAVID, PLEASE LOOK AT ME!

BOTH.

    THAT SOMETIME JUST HAPPENS TO BE NOW.

    (She takes her satchel.)

DAVID. What's that?

GABRIELLE. My things.

DAVID. You going somewhere?

GABRIELLE. I'm going away.

DAVID. Gabrielle –

GABRIELLE. Don't say anything, David.

DAVID. Don't say anything? O.K. I'll just stand here dumb.

GABRIELLE. You knew sooner or later I'd move on.

DAVID. I didn't know that.

GABRIELLE. You can't just dance in New Rochelle all your
    life –

DAVID. Who ever said you have to do that?

GABRIELLE. David, I've got this clock inside me –

DAVID. Is that what you got inside you? Look, I feel like you just got here. We really hardly know each other. There's a lot about me I haven't told you. Some thrilling stuff ... I'm not going to beg you.

GABRIELLE. Good.

DAVID. All right I'll beg. Stay!

GABRIELLE. David, this has nothing to do with you.

DAVID. That's fine. Great. Who does it have to do with?

GABRIELLE. It has to do with me. I gotta find out what's out there for me. I've gotta go

Music 10: WHEN I AM MOVIN'

WHEN I AM MOVIN'
WHEN I'M IN THE AIR
I DON'T REALLY CARE WHAT'S BELOW
WIN, LOSE, I CHOOSE THE SHOW.

WHEN I AM MOVIN'
WHEN I'M NOT HELD DOWN
THEN I GO TO TOWN IN THE SKY
NO CROWDS, JUST CLOUDS AND I.

TAKE IT FOR WHAT IT'S WORTH
MAYBE I'LL FALL TO EARTH CRASHING
BUT I WON'T WALK AWAY
'TIL I HEAR PEOPLE SAY, "SMASHING!"

WHEN I AM MOVIN'
WHEN I AM IN FLIGHT
NOTHING IS QUITE LIKE BEFORE
I'M NOT AFRAID ANYMORE.

I NEED A CHANCE TO FLY
I NEED A DANCE TO TRY MY WAY
DAVID, I HEAR A DRUM
MAKING ME DANCE ON SOME HIGHWAY!

I WON'T BE FALLING APART HERE
THOUGH I MAY LEAVE HALF MY HEART HERE.

WHEN I AM MOVIN'
MY SPIRIT CAN SOAR

AND I CAN EXPLORE THE UNKNOWN
I NEED SOME TIME ON MY OWN.

THIS IS THE WAY I AM
NO ONE CAN SAY I AM LYING
THERE'S NOT A SOUL TO BLAME
WHEN I WAS BORN, I CAME FLYING!

WHEN I AM MOVIN'
I WON'T BE HELD BACK
I'LL STAY ON THE TRACK 'TIL I DIE
IT'S MY SHOT
AND I'VE GOT TO FLY!

DAVID. I love you.

GABRIELLE. You promised you'd never say that.

DAVID. Well, you know me – I break my promises. I love you.

(She picks up a few other things, looking a little over-loaded.)

You can't just pick up and go like this.

(Searching for something else to say.)

You owe me rent.

GABRIELLE. I'll leave my Buddha here for you.

DAVID. Stay a few more days –

GABRIELLE. Good-bye, David.

DAVID. Where you going?

GABRIELLE. LA.

DAVID. L.A.? Alone?

GABRIELLE. Well, there's this guy –

DAVID. A guy, oh.

GABRIELLE. Look, it doesn't mean anything.

DAVID. Well, that's a relief.

GABRIELLE. We met in class. He knows some people on the coast. Look I told you from the start I didn't want anything meaningful or lasting.

DAVID. Well, there's nothing meaningful about this! It's cheap and insignificant! I just happen to be crazy about it!

GABRIELLE. I gotta go –

DAVID. *(Calling after her.)* Maybe if you stood still awhile –

GABRIELLE. *(Turning to him.)* I don't wanna stand still! I get afraid when I stand still!

Music 10a: Reprise – WHEN I AM MOVIN'

WHEN I AM MOVIN'
I WON'T BE HELD BACK
I'LL STAY ON THE TRACK TIL I DIE
IT'S MY SHOT
AND I'VE GOT TO FLY!

(She leaves.)

Music 10b: WHEN I AM MOVIN' – Chaser

Scene 11: David's Apartment

*(**DAVID** is alone onstage.)*

DAVID. No, I'm not going to let this get to me. I'm going to be O.K. I don't need her. Monday night at Krazy Korn I'll show 'em. I'll let them know a brilliant new comic has arrived. I'll be funny and charming. And afterwards, gorgeous models will be hanging on my arms. I'll be written up in People magazine. I'll have a guest spot on "Live at Five." Barbara Walters will do a special on me.

Music 11: THINK BIG

I'LL GO FOR THE SILK AND THE SUEDE
AND I'M GONNA THINK BIG
WHY CAN'T I GO FOR THE JADE
|I'M GONNA THINK BIG
PEOPLE ARE JUST SO AFRAID
THAT THEY TAKE WHAT THEY'RE GIVEN
BUT THAT ISN'T LIVIN'
I WANT THE WHOLE TREE NOT A TWIG
OH, I'M ON THE BRINK
I'M NOT GONNA SINK
'CAUSE I'M GONNA ONLY THINK BIG!

(He comes forward.)

IF I'VE GOT A CHOICE
I'LL TAKE A ROLLS ROYCE
AND LEAVE GIRLS LIKE HER FAR BEHIND
GIRLS ARE SO EASY TO FIND
I'LL GO FOR THE BEST AND THROW OUT THE REST

I WANT TO HAVE LUNCH AT LE CIRQUE
AND I'M GONNA DRINK BIG
MAYBE YOU THINK I'M BERSERK
BUT I'M GONNA THINK BIG
NOBODY EVERY GETS FAR
IF THEY WISH FOR A LITTLE
OR ACT NON-COMMITTAL
I WANT TO TAKE MORE THAN A SWIG

AND I'LL SIGN IT IN INK
AND I DON'T NEED A SHRINK
'CAUSE HE'D ONLY TELL ME THINK BIG!

(He dances, the glamour of the world coming alive for him as everything else fades.)

GIVE ME A PENTHOUSE ON PARK
I'M GONNA THINK BIG
DINNER IN SPAIN ON A LARK
'CAUSE I'M GONNA THINK BIG
WHY SHOULD I JUST TAKE A STAR
WHEN I WANT THE WHOLE PLANET
DON'T NEED GABBY OR JANET
THERE'LL BE TEN OTHER GIRLS THAT I'LL DIG
NOT A THING OUT OF SYNCH
MY LIFE'S IN THE PINK
'CAUSE I'M GONNA ONLY THINK BIG!

END ACT I

Music 12: ENTR'ACTE

ACT II

Scene 1: Krazy Korn Klub

M.C. Let's give a real Krazy Korn welcome to – David Ackerman!

(A few isolated claps as a spotlight comes up on **DAVID,** *wearing a Krazy Korn T-shirt. He is tentative, unsure of himself.)*

DAVID. Thank you. Thanks a lot. Thanks. Thanks, really. I know it's past most of your bedtimes. Actually, it's past my bedtime ... You know it's not easy being a comic. I had to get a day job to kinda supplement my comedy income. And my comedy income is truly a comedy. It's an interesting job. I work for one of the local radio stations here. What I do is get in my car during rush hour and ride around and report on helicopter traffic ...

(Beat)

Show of hands. Who among you is listening to me and who's faking it?

(Singing)

"IT HAD TO BE YOU – "

(Beat)

Remember the old days when you could actually sing along with music?

(He's trying to keep his courage up.)

Comedy isn't the only thing I do. I tried a lot of other things. I got so desperate once I took an occupational-aptitude test. They told me, based on the results, I should be a shepherd. Not a bad job. Three-fifty an hour, a couple of good-looking sweaters. But let me tell you, it's tough getting all those sheep across Times Square. Especially on days when it's alternate-side-of-the-sheep parking.

(Beat)

Last night I had this incredible dream that comedians were in demand. In fact, there was a great scarcity of them – because a plague had wiped out all the comedians east of the Mississippi, just the comedians, mind you. Everyone else was spared. Lucky me —I was in the midst of a giant depression. It got the telephone company – a real laugh riot. And my dentist, Sam Chen – "famous mouth humorist" – fell like a ton of bricks. So did the shrinks. Never met a shrink that didn't break me up. I got a shrink. He's a riot. Keeps saying, "David, you're important. Tell me about yourself." And when I do, he falls asleep.

(Beat)

Thanks. You been a good audience. Gimme a call sometime. I'm also available for wakes and funerals.

(The act is over. A waiter comes out and begins to clean up.)

WAITER. Closin' time, pal

(Looks at the money on the bar.)

Geez, would ya look at this. Buncha cheapskates in here tonight. Hey, caught yer act.

(Repeating David's punch line.)

"Alternate-side-of-the-sheep parking."

(Laughs)

DAVID. Oh, so you're the one that laughed.

WAITER. Hey, wanna beer?

DAVID. Got any hemlock?

WAITER. Lite or regular?

(Gives him a beer.)

DAVID. Thanks.

WAITER. So how long you been a comic?

DAVID. Let's see. What time is it?

(He looks at his watch; **WAITER** *laughs.)*

WAITER. A lot of the big guys bombed out in the beginning. It's part of the turf. Well, I gotta lock up, pal.

(He goes. As **DAVID** *sings, he makes his way back to his piano.)*

Music 13: *LATE NITE COMIC*

DAVID.

> STAY UP AT THE DINER HALF THE NIGHT
> TRY YOUR BEST TO GET THE NEW BIT RIGHT
> BUT THE JOKES ARE THE WORST
> AND THE COMIC RIGHT BEFORE YOU SAYS HE
> WROTE THE WHOLE THING FIRST
> AND THREW IT OUT.

> CALL THE CLUB AND ASK THEM FOR A SPOT
> THEY SAY THREE A.M. IS ALL WE GOT
> BUT YOU SAY YOU DON'T CARE
> AND SURE ENOUGH A WAITRESS IS THE
> ONLY PERSON THERE
> AND SHE WALKS OUT.

> LATE NITE COMIC, YOUR AUDIENCE IS GONE
> BUT STILL YOU GRAB THAT MICROPHONE AND
> STILL YOU CARRY ON
> LATE NITE COMIC, KEEP THE LAUGHTER COMING
> TIL THE DAWN.

> YOU END UP AS THE LAST ONE ON THE SHOW
> SEVEN HECKLERS TELL YOU WHERE TO GO
> AND YOU WISH YOU WERE DEAD
> 'CAUSE WHEN YOU GET OFF STAGE THE OWNER
> QUICKLY TURNS HIS HEAD
> AND WALKS AWAY.

LATE NITE COMIC, YOUR AUDIENCE IS GONE
BUT STILL YOU GRAB THAT MICROPHONE
AND STILL YOU CARRY ON
LATE NITE COMIC, KEEP THE LAUGHTER COMING
TIL THE DAWN
LATE NITE COMIC LATE NITE COMIC LATE NITE
COMIC
NEVER YAWN ... NEVER YAWN.

So I was back at the piano.

(He plays.)

Was I going to let one little setback get to me? No. Next day I was back in the swim of things.

(He picks up the phone; bright.)

Hey, Jake, David Ackerman here. You remember. You said call next week –

(Spelling it.)

A.-C-K-E-R-M-A-N. I told you that story about the two midgets. Had you rolling on the floor .. hello?

(Front)

Funny thing about rejection. It's like a drug. Once you try it, you just can't get enough of it.

(On the phone.)

I was in last week, Mr. Kalodny. I was the funny guy. Your cook was crazy about me –

(He stops; listens.)

What? You can use me? Friday?

(Front)

He wants me.

(Continuing on the phone.)

The two a.m. slot? Does it interest me? Yes, it interests me!

Music 13a: *Reprise – STAND UP*

AND I'M THROWIN' OUT ALL MY SONGBOOKS NOW
'CAUSE I'M GONNA BE A STAND UP
I DON'T NEED THAT STUFF 'CAUSE I MADE A VOW
THAT I'M GONNA BE A STAND UP
AND I GOT THAT SPOT ON A FRIDAY NIGHT
AND I WILL KEEP BUILDING THAT DEMAND UP
AND YOU'LL NEVER CATCH ME WHEN I'M SITTING
DOWN
'CAUSE I'M GONNA BE A STAND UP

STAND UP!
STAND UP!
STAND UP!

Scene 2: Mr. Rib's Club

Music 13b: PLAY ON

(**DAVID** *wears a Mr. Rib's T-shirt. An M.C. introduces him.*)

M.C. And now, let's hear it for David Ackerman!

(**DAVID** *performs, more relaxed than he has been in the past. He is beginning to be at home with his profession. He talks easily with his audience, as though they were old friends. He may even go into the house.*)

DAVID. Nobody holds hands anymore. To me, hand-holding is one of the essentials of life. You hold someone's hand – you know in a flash your whole relationship with them. Try it. Go on. Take hold of the person's hand next to you. It's O.K., I give my permission. Yeah, even you. Go on. Grab a hand. O.K., now relax. Let your imagination go free. Made a mistake, didn't you? That wasn't who you should have been out with tonight.

(*He goes back onto the stage.*)

I didn't sleep well last night. I kept thinking about my girlfriend. A dancer. Maybe you seen one of her concerts. She gave one last month in the Lexington Avenue subway during rush-hour. Terrific girl, though. Very lively. She could get high on a can of peaches ... We met in a piano bar. One of those places people who don't know who they are go to hoping to forget they don't know who they are. She was running from this guy. We had a little collision. I said, "Hi." She said, "Hi." We realized immediately we had a lot in common. So I invited her to live with me. She arrived with a Buddha, a poster of herself when she's three and a tutu. I mean who could resist incentives like that?

I used to be this easy-going guy. I loved to smell flowers. Listen to "love songs, nothing but love songs." But then I realized nobody gets ahead in this world without night sweats, morning angst and the blahs. You gotta suffer. I mean, who knows, maybe the secret to long life is "worry." "Having trouble sleeping? Try – worry." "Forget that face lift. Worry." I wasn't going to be left out. I shed my easy-going ways and entered into the world of – bad relationships. I've made a career of them. In fact, when people ask me what I do, I say, "I do bad relationships." When friends say, "Hey, David, why don't you come for dinner tonight?" I say, "Would love to. Can I bring my bad relationship?" "Sure, love to meet her. Is she as bad as the last one?" "Worse." Problem is – now that she's gone, I keep imagining I see her everywhere. I was in a yoga class the other day and there she was chanting next to me. I reached over to touch her – turns out to be a ninety-year-old guru with shingles. I was doing a gig at the Yuk Club over on Jericho Turnpike — there she was sipping on a pina colada. I said, "Surprise!" – turns out to be a three hundred pound bricklayer. I told my shrink about her. And now he thinks he's seeing her. Yesterday I followed her into a Pizza Hut, a sperm bank and a nautilus center. Finally the woman turned and looked at me. It was a nun.

Music 14: OBSESSED

OBSESSED!
I HAVE TRIED A THOUSAND TIMES TO GET IT OFF MY CHEST
OBSESSED!
I AM ALWAYS COMING BACK AGAIN FOR ONE MORE TEST
YOU WOULD THINK THAT I WOULD LEARN FROM ALL MY TRIES
BUT IT SEEMS I THRIVE ON HEARING THOSE GOODBYES
OBSESSED!
OBSESSED!
OBSESSED!

INSANE!

I MUST SURELY BE A GLUTTON FOR THE HURT AND
PAIN
INSANE!
I TELL ALL MY FRIENDS I'M SO IN LOVE AND THEN
COMPLAIN
I HAVE FOUND THE PERFECT GIRL FOR ME AGAIN
ON THE DAY THAT SHE IS SWEARING OFF OF MEN
INSANE!
INSANE!
I'M INSANE!

(He sits, as if he is finished, then immediately jumps back up.)

OBSESSED!
I AM ABSOLUTELY POSITIVE I NEED A REST
OBSESSED!
YOU WILL NEVER CATCH ME LOOKING AT ANOTHER
BREAST
I AM GOING OUT TO PROBABLY GET DRUNK
BETTER YET I THINK I'M GONNA BE A MONK
OBSESSED!
OBSESSED!
I'M OBSESSED!

(He leaves, then immediately returns.)

OBSESSED!
WHEN I THINK OF ALL THE TIME AND TROUBLE I
INVEST
OBSESSED!
I'VE BEGUN TO THINK I'M BETTER OFF WHEN I STAY
DRESSED
DON'T SUGGEST TO ME TO CHANGE THE OTHER
WAY
'CAUSE I'D EVEN BE OBSESSED WITH BEING GAY
OBSESSED!
OBSESSED!
I'M OBSESSED!

Thanks, you been terrific.

Scene 3: A Bar

(**DAVID** *is alone onstage.*)

DAVID. She was taking over my life. And she wasn't even around to share the pain. I decided the only way to get rid of her was to replace her. I'd find somebody new. I combed the city. I mean, she's out there. She had to be. I did a round of bars and clubs. I was gonna let her know right off what I wanted.

(*Calling*)

Bartender, yo!

(*He drinks his drink; looks about; spots a* **YOUNG WOMAN**. *There is a soft, bluesy, sexy musical underscore playing as* **DAVID** *speaks to the* **WOMAN**.)

I'm looking for a permanent relationship.

(*She turns to him*)

I wanna go to museums together – and join video clubs together – and take weekend hikes together – and jog together – and eat macrobiotic together. I wanna have kids – and a dog. And a steady job – real work — nine to five work. So what do you say?

WOMAN. God, I wish you'd come five minutes ago. You see that guy over there? He said the same things to me. We're goin' back to his place to talk it over. Look, if it don't work out, I'll be back here tomorrow.

(*She turns away.*)

DAVID. (*Calling*) Bartender, yo!

(*He takes another drink for courage. He sees a* **SECOND WOMAN**.)

Look, I'm a lonely guy. I lost my girl. I can't hold a job. I'm in intensive therapy, but we're boring ourselves to death. I have a palpitating heart. And my head's playing tricks on me. But I thought with a loving woman, a woman not unlike yourself —1 could get back on track. So what d'you say?

SECOND WOMAN. You are one sick puppy.

(She turns away.)

DAVID. *(Calling)* Yo! Bartender! Make it a double!

(He takes another, larger drink. He turns to yet a **THIRD WOMAN** *— tall, sexy, dressed in Frederick's of Hollywood style.)*

Hello! Wanna join the party?

THIRD WOMAN. *(Turning to him.)* You talkin' to me?

DAVID. *(Front)* Was I hallucinating?

THIRD WOMAN. Let's have a taste of that.

(She throws back his drink.)

Delilah's the name.

DAVID. Delilah — really?

THIRD WOMAN. What do they call you?

DAVID. I'm ... Samson.

(Front)

Was this the woman for me?

THIRD WOMAN. Samson, what do you say we get to know each other better?

DAVID. Sounds O.K. to me.

(Front)

God moves in mysterious ways.

THIRD WOMAN. You're just what I've been looking for.

(She moves in on him; she hands him a joint.)

Music 15: *RELAX WITH ME, BABY*

DO I MAKE YOU NERVOUS?
DO I MAKE YOU SHAKE?
ARE YOU SO AFRAID
THAT YOUR HEART IS GONNA BREAK?
WELL, JUST RELAX WITH ME, BABY
RELAX WITH ME, BABY
YOU'LL BE ALL RIGHT, YEAH
'CAUSE IF YOU AIN'T RELAXED NOW
YOU WILL BE BY THE END OF THE NIGHT.

(SECOND WOMAN *appears.)*

SECOND WOMAN.

> NOW I SEE YOU SMOKIN'
> THOSE FUNNY CIGARETTES
> BUT IF YOU PUT IT OUT NOW
> YOU WON'T HAVE NO REGRETS.
> WELL, JUST RELAX WITH ME, BABY
> RELAX WITH ME, BABY
> YOU'LL BE ALL RIGHT, YEAH
> 'CAUSE IF YOU AIN'T RELAXED NOW
> YOU WILL BE BY THE END OF THE NIGHT.

> *(They are all over him.* **FIRST WOMAN** *appears.)*

FIRST WOMAN.

> NOW VODKA AND TONICS
> ARE ALL RIGHT FOR STARTERS
> BUT WAIT 'TIL YOU SEE
> WHAT COMES WITH THESE GARTERS.

> *(She wraps her leg around 'him.)*

> SO PUT DOWN THAT COCKTAIL
> AND PUT UP YOUR FEET
> I FOUND A PLACE
> WHERE THE BOTH OF US CAN MEET.

THREE WOMEN.

> WELL, JUST RELAX WITH ME, BABY
> RELAX WITH ME, BABY
> YOU'LL BE ALL RIGHT, YEAH
> 'CAUSE IF YOU AIN'T RELAXED NOW
> YOU WILL BE BY THE END OF THE NIGHT.

> *(***ONE OF THE WOMEN*** rips off his shirt.)*

THIRD WOMAN.

> NOW LET ME GET CLOSER
> AND I'LL LET YOU SEE SOME
> AND THEN IF YOU'RE GOOD
> WE MIGHT TRY A THREESOME.

> *(He takes a gulp of his drink.* **SECOND WOMAN** *takes it from him.)*

SECOND WOMAN.

SO GIVE ME AN HOUR
BETTER YET GIVE ME TWO
AND I'LL SHOW YOU THINGS
THAT NO ONE ELSE CAN DO.

THREE WOMEN.
WELL, JUST RELAX WITH ME, BABY
RELAX WITH ME, BABY
YOU'LL BE ALL RIGHT, YEAH
'CAUSE IF YOU AIN'T RELAXED NOW
YOU WILL BE BY THE END OF THE NIGHT
'CAUSE IF YOU AIN'T RELAXED NOW
YOU WILL BE BY THE END OF THE NIGHT.

Scene 4: A Dressing Room

(In a very compact dressing room, **DAVID** *is preparing to do his act. He puts on a Rascals T-shirt.)*

DAVID. *(Front)* What can you say about debauchery? It's got its place, I suppose. It kind of wakes you up to realities. The truth of the matter is – it leaves you spent.

(A **COMIC** *comes in.)*

COMIC. You're on next.

*(***DAVID*** nods affirmatively.)*

DAVID. I'm working this new club. They've had me back three times. The audiences are small, but enthusiastic.

COMIC. They're dyin' out there. I could hear them decomposing.

DAVID. *(Front)* The place is called Rascals. It's gonna cost me more to get out here than they're paying me.

COMIC. Table three's really hostile.

DAVID. *(Front)* Still I'm dreaming Dangerfield's, I'm dreaming Vegas, I'm dreaming Carson, but I'm happy for fifteen minutes out on 1-95.

COMIC. See ya, killer.

(He goes. **DAVID** *rises.)*

DAVID. As for Gabrielle, I think I've gotten her out of my system. I actually hadn't thought of her for two hours.

(A **BUSBOY** *comes in.)*

BUSBOY. Your name Ackerman?

DAVID. Yeah.

BUSBOY. Phone call.

DAVID. *(Crossing to the phone.)* My agent, probably. Got me booked in the Persian Gulf.

(He picks up the phone.)

Hello.

(Lights up on a distraught **GABRIELLE** *at a phone booth.)*

GABRIELLE. Hello ... David? David?

DAVID. *(Front)* My imagination was definitely playing tricks on me.

(Into the phone.)

Gabby – ?

GABRIELLE. Hi, David.

DAVID. It's really you?

GABRIELLE. I'm sorry to bother you –

DAVID. What is it? What's the matter?

GABRIELLE. Nothing, I just ...

DAVID. Is something wrong?

GABRIELLE. David, I ..

DAVID. What's going on? Where are you? L.A.?

GABRIELLE. No. I'm uptown on Third Avenue.

DAVID. Third Avenue? What are you doing on Third Avenue?

GABRIELLE. David – things aren't happening like I planned. There are no violins. Or follow spots. Or men with bouquets –

GABRIELLE. David, I ...

DAVID. Look, stay where you are. No – go over to Bloomingdale's. Stand in front of Bloomingdale's.

GABRIELLE. I don't wanna go to Bloomingdale's.

DAVID. Go to Bloomingdale's. I'll take a taxi there.

GABRIELLE. David –

DAVID. I'll be there in no time. Just go there.

GABRIELLE. David — ?

DAVID. What is it?

GABRIELLE. Do you still love me?

BUSBOY. *(Calling)* Hey, mister, you're on!

DAVID. *(Into phone.)* Go to Bloomingdale's.

(He hangs up; to BUSBOY.)

Cover for me.

BUSBOY. Cover for you? I'm the busboy.

DAVID. Don't worry. They'll never know the difference!

Scene 5: The Steps in Front of David's Apartment

(**DAVID** *is alone onstage.*)

DAVID. I stood in front of Bloomingdale's three hours. She never showed. I began having conversations with the mannikins.

(*To the mannikins.*)

"Love the jacket, pal, but the slacks are a little bizarre." And that wouldn't have been so bad if the stiffs didn't start talking back to me. I went home – determined to put her out of my mind forever this time –

(*Lights up on* **GABRIELLE** *sitting on the steps in front of David's apartment.*)

GABRIELLE. Hi, David.

DAVID. (*Front*) And there she was sitting on my front steps – looking like the Little Flower Girl.

GABRIELLE. Do I?

DAVID. What?

GABRIELLE. Look like the Little Flower Girl?

DAVID. Where the hell were you? I waited in front of Bloomingdale's all night. I missed my spot at the club –

GABRIELLE. I'm sorry.

DAVID. Sorry – terrific.

GABRIELLE. I didn't know if you really wanted to see me.

DAVID. Really wanted to see you? You call me. You sound like you're in trouble –

GABRIELLE. I'm O.K. now

(*She looks at him; he sits next to her.*)

DAVID. You look terrible.

GABRIELLE. I know. I haven't slept in two days. Everything's out of whack, David. L.A. was a big mistake.

DAVID. Oh, yeah?

GABRIELLE. I didn't fit in. I felt like I had two heads or something.

DAVID. You do have two heads. This one's terrific — the one that flies around on a broomstick I'm not so sure of.

GABRIELLE. I'm serious.

DAVID. So am I.

GABRIELLE. Here you know nobody likes you. You walk down the street – you feel it. You talk to people – you know it. In L.A. they smile at you. They're interested. They're passionate about you. And the next time they see you, they don't even know your name. Of course, if your name's Linda Evans, maybe they know your name?

DAVID. So change your name to Linda Evans.

GABRIELLE. I just may do that ... I'm thinking maybe I should become a nun.

DAVID. You'd make a terrific nun.

GABRIELLE. You really think so?

DAVID. You'd revolutionize the church.

GABRIELLE. I always liked nuns. They're great-looking women. My favorite was Sister Rachel in the third grade. She was beautiful. She got pregnant and got married.

(She looks at him.)

You know what I missed most about you?

DAVID. I'm almost afraid to hear.

GABRIELLE. You made me laugh when we made love.

DAVID. I made you laugh?

GABRIELLE. Yeah. The first time I thought – this guy's weird. But then I began to like it. And then I began to think — this guy's on to something. You're a funny man.

DAVID. *(After a brief pause.)* So what's next for you?

GABRIELLE. I don't know ... I don't know. I know I'm a child, David. The Ballet is so real to me. It's my whole life. I know I'll never be a great dancer. I'll never dance at the Metropolitan Opera. I'll never be Margot Fonteyn. There'll just be a lot of one-night stands and sore feet.

DAVID. Gabby, you're a dancer. You don't need anyone to tell you that. 'Cause finally it doesn't matter. Believe me, I know. You've got to dance. Dance anywhere. Dance on a street corner. Dance in a subway. But dance.

GABRIELLE. *(After brief pause.)* I missed your bed. Some beds don't feel right, you know. But your bed – we were like instant friends. Look, I know it's not fair of me barging in on you like this.

DAVID. Who's complaining? You hear me complaining?

GABRIELLE. Well, complain. Complain, David.

DAVID. Stop barging in on me like this! Goddamit, stay out of my life! Stay away from me!

(**GABRIELLE** *breaks down in tears.*)

Hey, I'm kidding. I'm kidding.

(He holds her.)

It's good to see you. It's good to hold you.

GABRIELLE. Can I come home?

Music 16: **GABRIELLE** *– Reprise*

DAVID. Of course you can come home. Go put your things away.
GABRIELLE, YOU'LL ALWAYS HAVE A PLACE HERE
GABRIELLE, I LOVE TO SEE YOUR FACE HERE
GABRIELLE, I'LL ALWAYS LEAVE A LIGHT ON
NO ONE ELSE CAN BRING THE NIGHT ON HALF AS WELL ...
OH, GABRIELLE.

(She goes into the apartment.)

Scene 6: The Metropolitan Opera House

(**DAVID** *is alone onstage.*)

DAVID. So we were back together again. But it was different. There weren't the highs and the lows. We were polite. And very careful of each other's feelings. She took classes. I worked on routines. We took walks. Not as many as we used to. And we held hands. Sometimes. It's like we were working at being normal people. I had to do something to change things –

Music 16a: TO THE MET

(**DAVID** *leads* **GABRIELLE** *on blindfolded.*)

GABRIELLE. Where are you taking me?

DAVID. Will you trust me?

GABRIELLE. I trust you. Just where are you taking me?

(He removes the blindfold.)

What's this?

DAVID. The Met.

GABRIELLE. It's not.

DAVID. It is.

GABRIELLE. *(Loudly)* The Metropolitan Opera House?

DAVID. Shhh!

GABRIELLE. What are we doing here?

DAVID. I borrowed it.

GABRIELLE. You borrowed the Met?

DAVID. For fifteen minutes.

GABRIELLE. You crazy?

DAVID. You can dance here.

GABRIELLE. Dance?

(She looks at him.)

Look, before we get in big trouble –

DAVID. There's no trouble.

(Calling)

George!

(To **GABRIELLE**.*)*

I know the house manager. It's a favor. For three hundred bucks he snuck us in.

GABRIELLE. Where'd you get three hundred bucks?

DAVID. I hocked my piano.

GABRIELLE. You did what?

DAVID. Who needs a piano?

(Calling again.)

George!

(He calls again)

George! Could we have a light up here?

(A spotlight hits **GABRIELLE**.*)*

There!

(He gives her a flower.)

For you!

(He looks into the orchestra pit.)

Musicians!

(He goes and sits at the piano and plays.)

O.K., it's not a hundred violins. It's too many violins anyway.

(He calls out.)

Presenting for the first time on the stage of the Metropolitan Opera House – Gabrielle!

(She stands still.)

You're on. You only got thirteen minutes left! For God's sake — dance!

Music 17: DANCE

DANCE
YOU STARTED OUT AND DIDN'T HAVE A CHANCE
DANCE
YOU NEVER FOUND A WAY YOU COULD ADVANCE
BUT, GIRL, THE SPOTLIGHT'S ON YOU NOW
DON'T TELL ME THAT YOU'VE FORGOTTEN HOW

YOU'VE BEEN HANGING ON SO LONG
BUT YOU'VE ALWAYS BEEN SO STRONG
'CAUSE YOU'VE GOT WHAT IT TAKES AND YOU'LL
SURVIVE
YOU CANNOT GIVE UP THOSE TIGHTS
YOU WERE MADE FOR STAGE AND LIGHTS
SO GO AHEAD, IT'S TIME YOU CAME ALIVE

GABRIELLE.

DANCE
IT ALWAYS GIVES THE FEELING OF ROMANCE
DANCE
THE ONLY THING THAT LEAVES ME IN A TRANCE
AND WHAT COULD EVER TAKE ITS PLACE?
WHAT COULD EVER HAVE SUCH STYLE AND GRACE?

I'VE BEEN HANGING ON SO LONG
AND I USED TO BE SO STRONG
BUT NOW IT TAKES SO MUCH TO JUST SURVIVE
BUT IF I GIVE UP THESE TIGHTS
WELL, THERE'D BE ONE TOO MANY NIGHTS
THAT I'D BE WONDERIN' WHY I'M STILL ALIVE.

ONCE UPON A TIME
MY CINDERELLA DREAMS
WERE DREAMS OF BEING BALLET'S BIGGEST HIT
BUT ONCE THE BALL IS OVER
YOU WILL HEAR THE MUSIC FADE
AND THE TOE SHOE DOESN'T FIT.

DANCE
THE WORLD CAN ALWAYS NAME YOU AT A GLANCE
DANCE
YOU NEVER REALLY GET A SECOND CHANCE

BEFORE I'M LOST AMONG THE CROWD
LET ME DANCE WHERE I CAN FEEL SO PROUD ...
PROUD

(She begins to dance, imagining she is dancing with some elite company such as the American Ballet Theater. She could possibly be joined by apparitions of past dancers, which would fade as she concludes the dance.)

Music 17a: PLAY ON

Scene 7: David's Apartment

(**DAVID** *is alone onstage.*)

DAVID. We'd been together six weeks. I was actually becoming happy with our situation. She began doing nice things for me. She'd come to all my shows. Laugh at all my jokes. Even the ones she didn't get. We even began to eat normal food. One morning for breakfast we actually had oatmeal. O.K., there was chocolate syrup on top. But at least she was trying. And, best of all, I cured her of post-coital depression. I was beginning to think the good life was possible. I was certainly hoping we'd run out of goodbyes.

GABRIELLE. I'm going on tour.

DAVID. *(Front)* I should have known better.

GABRIELLE. I got this job. It's a small company. Actually, they're sort of improvisational. We go to Toledo, then a week in St. Louis, Pittsburgh, Kansas City –

DAVID. What are you talking about?

GABRIELLE. David, I've loved these last six weeks. Everything we've done together. You made me feel there was something in me worth noticing – worth loving. You gave me confidence. And you gave me the greatest gift in the world. A chance to dance at the Metropolitan Opera House. That's the most incredible thing anyone's ever done for me.

DAVID. I thought things were set between us.

GABRIELLE. That scares me. Being set.

DAVID. You said you were going to stay here and study.

GABRIELLE. You said, "Dance anywhere."

DAVID. I meant anywhere here. Dance here.

GABRIELLE. David, sometimes when I'm with you that's all I want. And then there's this other thing – this clock that says, "keep moving."

DAVID. Reset the clock, dammit.

GABRIELLE. I don't want to fight, David.

DAVID. Well, I do.

GABRIELLE. I want to part friends.

DAVID. Is that what we are – friends?

GABRIELLE. Forget me, David.

DAVID. Sure.

GABRIELLE. I mean it. Forget me. I'm a pinhead. And pinheads aren't like other people. Our bodies don't respond normally. Our heads don't respond normally. You want a normal girl.

DAVID. Don't tell me what I want. If I wanted a normal girl, I'd find a normal girl.

GABRIELLE. Good-bye, David.

DAVID. You're going now?

GABRIELLE. My bus leaves in an hour.

DAVID. You always do that. You wait until the last minute.

GABRIELLE. Maybe I didn't want to think about it. Maybe it's hard for me to say good-bye. Did you ever think of that?

DAVID. You know what I thought – in my stupidity – I thought things would work out different for us. I thought it'd be something special.

GABRIELLE. It is something special.

DAVID. Gabby, I want a house, a dog, kids –

GABRIELLE. Kids? You really see me as a mother?

(*They look at each other, not knowing what to say.*)

I'll be back in a few months –

DAVID. Don't come back, Gabby. If you're going now, go for good. Don't come in and out of my life anymore. Don't pop in. Don't call me. Don't write me. Just go.

GABRIELLE. (*After a brief pause.*) Is that really what you want?

DAVID. Yes.

(*She goes to the door, then turns back.*)

GABRIELLE. Good-bye.

(*She goes.*)

DAVID. (*Front*) I knew it was the last time I'd ever see her.

Scene 8: A Comedy Club

M.C. Ladies and gentlemen, we are proud to present the comedy of David Ackerman.

(**DAVID** *picks up the mike and performs.*)

DAVID. My shrink tells me it's unreasonable to want a perfect mate. I don't know, I think it's possible, I'm perfect. Why can't others be? All she'd have to do is be a combination of Bo Derek and Garbo. And Bardot. And Rambo. And Dumbo. Don't mind me. I'm a little shell-shocked tonight. No, I didn't fight in the war. But I had this girlfriend. Well, she was more like a sparring partner than a girlfriend. We went fifteen rounds. She knocked me out and left. She was a bit of a flake. Actually, she was more like a blizzard ... And now she's gone. What's that old joke? "A guy without a girl is like a fish without a bicycle." Why is it I keep seeing fish riding around on bicycles? Look, you go on. It's no calamity. Sure I miss a few things. Like Chinese food at four in the morning. And dancing in the streets –

Music 18: Reprise – LATE NITE COMIC

I DREAM ABOUT HER ALMOST EVERY NIGHT
TRY TO TELL MYSELF THAT I'M ALL RIGHT
BUT I'M BARELY ALIVE
AND SOMETIMES I STAY UP ALL NIGHT AND WATCH
THE DAY ARRIVE
AND FALL ASLEEP.

I WALK AROUND PRETENDING I CAN WALK
CALLING ALL MY FRIENDS UP JUST TO TALK
BUT IT'S ALWAYS THE SAME
I DO ALL THE TALKING BUT I CANNOT SAY HER NAME
AGAIN JUST YET

LATE NITE COMIC
THE GIRL I LOVE IS GONE
WHAT CAN BRING HER BACK AGAIN
AND MAKE ME CARRY ON?
LATE NITE COMIC
MAYBE SHE'LL BE BACK BEFORE THE DAWN.

FIN'LLY FOUND THE GIRL WHO MADE ME LAUGH
SOMEONE MADE ME WHOLE INSTEAD OF HALF
BUT IT'S OVER SO SOON
I FOUND HER IN THE MORNING BUT SHE LEFT BY
AFTERNOON
NOW IT'S THE NIGHT

LATE NITE COMIC
THE GIRL I LOVE IS GONE
WHAT CAN BRING HER BACK AGAIN
AND MAKE ME CARRY ON?
LATE NITE COMIC
MAYBE SHE'LL BE BACK BEFORE THE DAWN.
LATE NITE COMIC
LATE NITE COMIC
LATE NITE COMIC, CARRY ON.

(Unable to continue, he leaves the stage.)

Scene 9: A Small Las Vegas Club off the Strip

(A sleazy **VEGAS CHORUS** *comes out.)*

VEGAS CHORUS.
> AAH AAH AAH AAH DAVID
> AAH AAH AAH AAH DAVID
> HE'S BRILLIANT AND NEW NOW
> HE'S LONG OVERDUE NOW
> IT'S DAVID'S DEBUT NOW TONIGHT!

M.C. We are proud to present for the first time in Las Vegas
— David Ackerman!

> **(DAVID** *comes on wearing a red Vegas T-shirt, or span-
> gled jacket.)*

Music 19: IT'S SUCH A DIFFERENT WORLD

DAVID & (CHORUS).
> A DRESSING ROOM – THEY'LL ADD ONE   (AAH)
> BEFORE YOU NEVER HAD ONE   (OOH)
> THE WAITRESSES ALL KISS YOU   (AAH)
> BEFORE THEY'D ONLY HISS YOU   (SSSS)
> IT'S SUCH A DIFFERENT WORLD –
> THIS IS HEAVEN THAT WAS HELL.
> THE MICROPHONES WERE BROKEN   (AAH)
> FOR PAY YOU'D GET A TOKEN   (OOH)
> BUT YOU'VE GOT PERFECT SOUND NOW   (TESTING
> 1-2-3)
> TAKE CABS TO GET AROUND NOW
> IT'S SUCH A DIFFERENT WORLD –
> WHEN YOUR NAME THEY DON'T MISSPELL.   (D-A-V-
> I-D)
> AND THERE'S SUCH A CHANGE IN THE ATTITUDE
> YOU GET BETTER DRINKS AND BETTER FOOD   (OOH)
> AND THEY FEED YOU FIRST
> AND THEY AREN'T RUDE LIKE BEFORE.   (AAH, NOW
> THEY'RE SO POLITE)
> AND YOUR INTRODUCTIONS ARE DONE WITH CLASS
> THEY SAY –

GIRLS.

YOU'RE THE BEST
'STEAD OF SOMETHING CRASS

DAVID.

AND WHEN YOU LEAVE THE STAGE
THEY ALL WANT YOUR ASS BACK FOR MORE.

CLUB OWNERS.

AND BECAUSE WE'RE THE BEST IN THE BUSINESS
WE BELIEVED IN DAVID FROM THE VERY START
YES, YOU KNOW WE'RE THE BEST IN THE BUSINESS
AND YOU KNOW WE'RE ONLY IN IT FOR THE
ART!   (WE'RE ONLY IN IT FOR THE ART)

DAVID.

YOUR RELATIVES WANT TICKETS   (AAH)
BEFORE YOU JUST HAD RICKETS   (AAH)
THERE'S LINES AROUND THE BLOCK
NOW   (AAH, CLEAR AROUND THE BLOCK)

(He looks both ways, smiles ironically)

YOU WORK AROUND THE CLOCK NOW   (TICK TOCK
TICK TOCK)
IT'S SUCH A DIFFERENT WORLD –
WHEN THEY WANT THE THINGS YOU SELL

DAVID & CHORUS.

IT'S SUCH A DIFFERENT WORLD –

DAVID.

WHEN YOU'RE FIN'LLY DOING WELL!

AND YOU MAKE ENOUGH TO PAY INCOME
TAX   (OOH)
YOU CAN BUY A SUIT AT A STORE LIKE SAKS   (OOH)
AND IF ONE JOKE FAILS   (OOH)
YOU DON'T GET THE AXE AND GET OUT.   (AAH, NO
NOT LIKE BEFORE)

And I've been gambling for the first time. It doesn't
work for me. You play too much Blackjack, it starts to
affect your head. I played a couple of hours last night,
went into the restaurant, waitress said, "Coffee?" "Hit

me." "Eggs?" "Split 'em." "Juice?"

(He does the flat-hand motion which in poker means:)

"I'm good."

(Beat)

I guess though we're all here 'cause there's always the chance you'll win. And if you win, you feel like you're Frank Sinatra. Like you personally have brought the casino to its knees. And it doesn't matter how much you win. You could win a half dollar and walk away going, "That's fifty cents they'll never see again." 'Course then you go out on the street, hail a cab, tip the doorman a buck, and you're right back in the red.

(The **THREE CLUB OWNER** *appear.)*

DAVID & CHORUS.

AND YOU'RE ON THE BILL WITH THE BIGGEST NAMES
AND TO GET YOUR PAY, THEY DON'T DARE PLAY GAMES
AND YOU WON'T BE LEAVIN'
IF THIS IS WHAT FAME'S ABOUT. (WHAT'S IT ALL ABOUT)

DAVID.

IT'S JUST WHAT YOU'VE BEEN WISHIN' (IT'S JUST WHAT YOU'VE BEEN WISHIN')

CLUB OWNERS.

YOU DON'T NEED TO AUDITION (YOU DON'T NEED TO AUDITION)

DAVID.

GET JOBS ON REPUTATION (GET JOBS ON REPUTATION)
THE OWNER'S NO RELATION (THE OWNER'S NO RELATION)
IT'S SUCH A DIFFERENT WORLD –
WHEN THEY NOTICE WHO YOU ARE   (OOH)
IT'S SUCH A DIFFERENT WORLD –

GIRLS.

SUCH A DIFFERENT, DIFFERENT WORLD

DAVID.

    IT'S SUCH A DIFFERENT WORLD –
    WHEN YOU FIN'LLY REACH YOUR STAR!

GIRLS.

    D.A.V.I.D. YOU ARE A STAR

    (The star-light flickers and flickers, trying to turn on. It finally makes it.)

Scene 10: The Same Vegas Club

*(*DAVID *is alone onstage seated at the piano.)*

DAVID. Actually, it was a small club off the main strip. But the drinks were free, and the girls were plentiful. Did a whole tour of America. Maybe you saw me. I opened a new club in Kansas City. Did two college campuses. A State Fair. Not bad. Every now and then I like to sit down at the keyboard – just to remember the old days. My roots, so to speak.

I AM NOT YOUR PIANO MAN OR BILLY JOEL –

Haven't seen Gabrielle for nearly a year. I suppose an affair's not a thing that's meant to last. An affair by its very nature is meant to have an ending. Like a good story.

(He continues playing as **GABRIELLE** *appears.)*

GABRIELLE. I read lips.

DAVID. What?

GABRIELLE. You were talking to yourself. *(He turns to her.)*

DAVID. Gabby!

GABRIELLE. I'm glad to see you.

DAVID. *(Front)* I don't believe this.

   (To **GABRIELLE.** *)*

What are you doing in Vegas?

GABRIELLE. Dancing.

DAVID. Dancing?

GABRIELLE. I'm with this fantastic company. Really first-rate. Well, actually, second-rate. But they do some very innovative things.

(She sits next to him.)

I saw your picture outside. It almost knocked me over. I said, "It's David. It's really David."

(She looks up.)

Oh-oh.

DAVID. What is it?

GABRIELLE. You see that guy over there?

DAVID. The one with the mean-looking face. My God, is he your date?

GABRIELLE. David, this is no time for jokes. That's Jose Barcelona.

DAVID. Jose Barcelona?

GABRIELLE. The famous revolutionary.

DAVID. Gabrielle, what the hell's going on?

GABRIELLE. I got him mixed up with this Latin choreographer. We were playing one of the smaller towns. We played towns you wouldn't even call towns. Anyway, someone pointed him out to me. At least I thought they were pointing him out. Actually, they were pointing someone else out. God, it's good to see you. You look so healthy. So robust.

DAVID. *(Front)* You probably think this is a fantasy –

GABRIELLE. Don't tell them that.

(Front)

This isn't a fantasy.

DAVID. *(Front)* It's a dream or something.

GABRIELLE. *(Front)* Don't listen to him.

DAVID. *(Front)* Or this time I really flipped out.

GABRIELLE. *(Front)* He hasn't flipped out. And things like this really do happen. And the fact we're together is just the most terrific thing in the world.

(To **DAVID.***)*

Look, I don't wanna mess things up for you. If it's going to be a problem.

DAVID. What problem?

GABRIELLE. About me moving in for awhile –

DAVID. Moving in?

GABRIELLE. I have no luggage. I lost most of it in the last town we were in – Don't say anything. Let's just stay here and think things through. We don't have to make any quick decisions. You thinking?

DAVID. I'm thinking.

GABRIELLE. Maybe certain people are just destined to be together – like there was some sort of planetary pull – like it doesn't matter what they do, where they go – they'll always be somehow beautifully stuck together – like Popeye and Olive Oyl. Like Fred and Wilma.

DAVID. *(Front)* I don't know if I wanna laugh or cry.

Music 20: *FINALE*

GABRIELLE.
WELL, IT HAD TO HAPPEN SOMETIME
THERE'S NO TELLING WHEN

DAVID.
GABRIELLE – I DON'T KNOW WHERE YOU CAME
FROM, GABRIELLE ...

GABRIELLE. *(Stopping him.)* No, stop. Stop. It's Yvonne.

DAVID. Yvonne?

(Front)

I wanna laugh.

GABRIELLE. It's got more mystery, don't you think? Yvonne. I see me in something satiny – tightly hugging my body. Maybe the hair falling over one eye.

DAVID.
OH, YVONNE, I DON'T CARE WHAT YOUR NAME IS
MY YVONNE, THE GIRL THAT YOU BECAME IS
MY YVONNE, IF GABBY DIDN'T FIT YOU THEN
PERHAPS THIS ONE WILL HIT YOU

EITHER WAY, I'D LOVE YOU IF I HAD TO CALL YOU
DON,
BUT I PREFER TO CALL YOU MY YVONNE,
I'M HAPPY THAT YOU BURST IN
YOU COULD QUENCH THIS ENDLESS THIRST INSIDE
MY HEART AGAIN
LET'S START AGAIN –

END ACT II

Music 21: BOWS

Music 22: EXIT MUSIC

Also by **Allan Knee**...

SHMULNIK'S WALTZ

Also by **Brian Gari**...

A HARD TIME TO BE SINGLE

Please visit our website **samuelfrench.com** for complete
descriptions and licensing information

READ THE BOOK ABOUT THE MUSICAL!

LISTEN TO THE CAST RECORDING!

Late Nite Comic composer/lyricist, Brian Gari, has produced an all star 20th anniversary edition of *Late Nite Comic* to benefit The Actors Fund and featuring Larry Hochman's original Broadway orchestrations.

The CD includes all cut songs and the performances of Broadway stars Brian D'Arcy James, Julia Murney, Karen Ziemba, Howard McGillin, Mary Testa, Liz Callaway, Chip Zien, Liz Larsen, Sal Viviano, Mario Cantone, Jason Graae, Paul Shaffer, Rupert Holmes, Tony Roberts, Daniel Reichard, Martin Vidnovic & Seth Rudetsky

This is the first time the songs have been heard with their original orchestrations since Broadway! The entire project was overseen by the show's composer/lyricist Brian Gari.

to purchase copies please visit
SAMUELFRENCH.COM

SING AND PLAY THE SONGS!

The *Late Nite Comic* piano/vocal selections songbook is now available in an all-new 20th Anniversary Edition, produced under the direction of Brian Gari by Alfred Publishing Co., Inc.

Expand your repertoire with piano/vocal sheet music for these show highlights: *Stand Up, Gabrielle, Clara's Dancing School, Late Nite Comic, It Had to Happen Sometime, When I'm Movin', Relax With Me Baby & Think Big.*

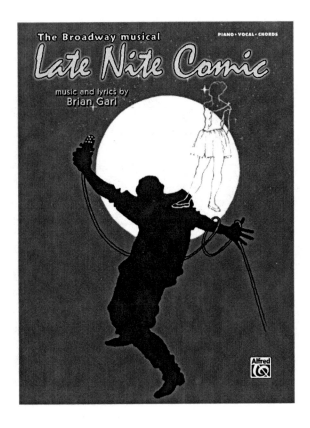

ADRIFT IN MACAO
Book and Lyrics by Christopher Durang
Music by Peter Melnick

Full Length / Musical / 4m, 3f / Unit Sets
Set in 1952 in Macao, China, *Adrift In Macao* is a loving parody of film noir movies. Everyone that comes to Macao is waiting for something, and though none of them know exactly what that is, they hang around to find out. The characters include your film noir standards, like Laureena, the curvacious blonde, who luckily bumps into Rick Shaw, the cynical surf and turf casino owner her first night in town. She ends up getting a job singing in his night club – perhaps for no reason other than the fact that she looks great in a slinky dress. And don't forget about Mitch, the American who has just been framed for murder by the mysterious villain McGuffin. With songs and quips, puns and farcical shenanigans, this musical parody is bound to please audiences of all ages.

Printed in the United States
202328BV00001B/127-198/P

9 780573 662423